Presented to

_____

by

_____

on

_____

45

Bedtime Bible Stories
for Little Ones

stories retold by Susan L. Lingo
illustrated by Kathy Parks

Standard Publishing
cincinnati, ohio

Standard Publishing, Cincinnati, Ohio
A division of Standex International Corporation

Text © 1999 by Susan L. Lingo
Art © 1999 by Standard Publishing
Sprout logo is a trademark of Standard Publishing.
All rights reserved
Printed in China
06 05 04   10 11 12 13

Project Editor: Laura Ring
Art Director: Coleen Davis
Graphic Arts: Mike Helm, Robert Korth
Editorial Support: Lise Caldwell, Jennifer Stewart, Leslie Durden
Production Director: Linda Ford
Director, Children's Products: Diane Stortz

Library of Congress Cataloging-in-Publication Data
Lingo, Susan L.
    My good night Bible / written by Susan Lingo ; illustrated by
Kathy Parks.
        p.   cm.
    Includes index.
    Summary : An illustrated collection of Bible stories for bedtime,
including activities, questions, prayers, and concepts to think
about just before sleep.
    ISBN 0-7847-0406-6
    1. Bible stories, English.   [1. Bible stories. 2. Prayer books
and devotions.]   I. Parks, Kathy (Kathleen D.), ill.   II. Title.
BS551.2.L49   1999
220.9'505--dc21   99-22435
                                                        CIP

Scriptures quoted from the *International Children's Bible, New Century Version*,
copyright © 1986, 1988 by Word Publishing, Dallas, Texas 75039. Used by permission.

from Susan

*For God and his perfect love that snuggles us all
like a warm nighttime blanket!
And for Lindsay and Dane—
you're never too old for a bedtime story!*

from Kathy

For Mrs. Haynes, who keeps me awake

Contents

Introduction 10

Old Testament

God Made the World *(Genesis 1:1–2:3)* 21

Adam Names the Animals *(Genesis 2:18-23; 3:20)* 25

Noah Obeys God *(Genesis 6:1–7:16)* 29

God's Promise *(Genesis 7:6–8:12)* 33

Noah Thanks God *(Genesis 8:13–9:17)* 37

The Oh-No Tower *(Genesis 11:1-9)* 41

Abraham Trusts God *(Genesis 12:1-9; 15:5, 6)* 45

A Baby for Sarah *(Genesis 18:1-15; 21:1-7)* 49

Baby in a Basket *(Exodus 2:1-10)* 53

Moses—God's Helper *(Exodus 3:1-15)* 57

Red Sea Run *(Exodus 14)* 61

God Gives Us What We Need *(Exodus 16)* 65

God's Ten Rules *(Deuteronomy 5)* 69

God Helps Joshua *(Joshua 6:1-20)* 73

Ruth and Naomi Are Friends *(Ruth 1)* 77

Samuel Listens to God *(1 Samuel 3)* 81

God Chooses David *(1 Samuel 16:1-13)* 85

David and Goliath *(1 Samuel 17:1-50)* 89

David Thanks God *(Psalm 23)* 93

Smart Solomon *(1 Kings 3:1-15)* 97

Daniel Prays *(Daniel 6)* 101

Brave Queen Esther *(Esther 4:9–5:8; 7)* 105

God Answers Jonah *(Jonah 1–3)* 109

New Testament

Happy Birthday, Jesus! *(Luke 2:4-7)* 115
Where's Jesus? *(Luke 2:41-52)* 119
Jesus Is Baptized *(Matthew 3:13-17)* 123
Follow-Me Fishermen *(Matthew 4:18-20)* 127
Love Everyone *(Matthew 5:43-48)* 131
Jesus Stops the Storm *(Luke 8:22-25)* 135
Dinner for 5,000 *(John 6:5-14)* 139
The Good Samaritan *(Luke 10:30-37)* 143
The Wise Builder *(Matthew 7:24-27)* 147
The Lost Sheep *(Luke 15:3-7)* 151
He Can Walk! *(Matthew 9:1-8)* 155
Jesus Loves Children *(Matthew 19:13-15)* 159
Zacchaeus Is Forgiven *(Luke 19:1-10)* 163
Give to God *(Luke 21:1-4)* 167
Jesus Is Coming! *(Matthew 21:6-11)* 171
Serve Each Other *(John 13:1-17; Mark 14:22-26)* 175
Jesus Died for Us *(Matthew 27:11-66)* 179
Jesus Is Alive! *(Luke 24:1-12)* 183
Tell Others About Jesus *(Mark 16:15-20)* 187
Hello, Holy Spirit! *(Acts 2)* 191
Prayer Helps Peter *(Acts 12:5-19)* 195
Our New Home *(Revelation 21:1–22:5)* 199

Scripture Index 204

Dear Parents
and Caregivers,

In the hustle-bustle of today's world, it's hard to find even a few moments of peace. Quiet times together with your children are scarce and fleeting. But these can be the most important times that you spend together, especially in those precious early years of your children's lives.

My Good Night Bible can help you make the most of the time that you have. Setting aside a special time to snuggle up and read Bible stories together is a wonderful way to let children know they are important and help them understand God's love. It also gives *you* a chance to remember what it's like to have the faith of a child and to be still and know God. This unhurried time shared with your child and God can be the most cherished part of your day!

What makes nighttime a great time for Bible stories?

By evening, most little children are winding down from the busy day, and "barely there" attention spans actually increase. The calm atmosphere provided by bedtime invites children to snuggle down and listen up.

At bedtime, you have a unique opportunity for you and your child to learn about God together. Afterwards, children have the whole night to "sleep on" God's Word! Educational studies have confirmed that sleeping or resting after learning a new skill, concept, or language actually increases understanding, retention, and recall. Reading God's Word and thinking about his truth at bedtime gives children the entire night to sleep with God-centered thoughts.

How can this book help?

With *My Good Night Bible,* you can develop a peaceful, calming bedtime routine that will help your child think about God while making an easy transition from busy day to silent night.

1. *Begin with the Bedtime Rhyme (page 16).* After toys are picked up, teeth are brushed, and pajamas are on, sing or say the Bedtime Rhyme to signal that story time is beginning.

2. *Choose a Bible story and read the "God said" or "Jesus said" Scripture verse together.* Each Bible verse presents the theme for that story, such as "Obey me" or "Forgive other people." These are verses that children can actually learn, understand, and put to use in their lives!

3. *Read the Bible story to your child.* One of the unique features of *My Good Night Bible* is the age-appropriate

storytelling. Each story uses short sentences and words that are familiar to a child's growing vocabulary. Alliteration, rhyme, and rhythm capture children's attention and invite them to repeat catchy story words and phrases.

4. *Look at the pictures. My Good Night Bible* is filled with lovingly designed illustrations that help bring the Bible to life for your child. "Find and point" picture activities located at the bottom of the story pages help focus your child's attention.

5. *Ask the story questions.* Our firefly friend, Night-Light, draws children even closer to the message with his simple questions.

6. *Talk to God together.* Use the prayer provided or pray in your own words. Let your child say a prayer of her own, too.

7. *Say the Sleep Time word.* Give your child a pleasant, God-centered thought to carry him through the night.

8. *Sing the Slumber Song (page 17).* Leave your child with the sound of your voice and the reminder of God's love.

Together-time tips for bedtime or anytime

Use these helpful hints and terrific tips to make learning about God more powerful and your together times more enjoyable.

- Take your time. Set aside the worries and duties of the day, slow down and just be with your child. Observe how many minutes it takes your child to get ready for quiet time. Be sure to allow enough "settling down" time—for both of you!

- Read bedtime stories in your child's bedroom. Tuck your child in bed, then cozy up close to share a Bible story. Reading bedtime stories in bed eliminates the awkward transition of going from some other room to the bedroom—and possibly "re-energizing" your child in the process!

- Create a soft, restful atmosphere. Use a small table lamp instead of distracting ceiling lights to illuminate the room. Invite your child to be the "Lamp Lighter" and allow her to turn the lamp on and off. The physical act of turning off the light will reinforce that it's quiet time and allows children to feel a sense of control. Remember, small night-lights give many children a sense of security and safety. If your child has a case of the bedtime blues caused by a darkened room, click on a cozy night-light!

- Invent your own Bible story review games. Help your child retain the Bible truths he is learning by creating clever review games and activities. Use the Scripture Index on page 204 to help you review the "God said" and "Jesus said" verses. See if your child can remember which story each verse is from, or simply read the verses and invite your child to be "Little Echo" and repeat them. Reread the story questions from a previous Bible story or visually review stories by hunting story pictures together. Look for ways to reinforce Bible stories with simple crafts, games, cooking activities, and songs.

- Have a special request night. One night a week, invite your child to choose her favorite Bible story to read together. The repetition is powerful and it demonstrates that you care about the things your child enjoys. For a twist, choose *your* favorite Bible story to share aloud!

- Develop a "choose it, then use it" habit. The day after a chosen Bible story is read, be on the lookout for ways to reinforce the biblical concept represented. For example, if you've just read the story "Give to God," ask your child to help you bake cookies to give to a neighbor. Explain that giving to others is a way of giving to God. Be sure to emphasize the "God said" or "Jesus said" Scripture verse during the day. Remember, Bible stories and concepts aren't just for reading—they're for living!

Share *My Good Night Bible* at bedtime, nap time, "cool-down" time—anytime you and your child want to experience the joy of learning about God's truth and love.

God bless you and sleep tight!

Susan Lingo

Hi, I'm Night-Light,
your special firefly friend!

If you look closely,
you will find me
in one of the pictures
of every story you read.
I love to read
Bible stories.
Let's read them
together!

Bedtime Rhyme

(to the tune of "Twinkle, Twinkle, Little Star")

Twinkle, twinkle, starry-shine,
(hold hands high and "twinkle" your fingers)

now it's Bible story time.
(hold hands side by side, like an open book)

We can learn of God above,
(point upward)

read of Jesus and his love.
(give yourself a hug)

Let's get ready right away
(move fists in circles in "hurrying" motion)

and be with God to end our day.
(hold hands in prayer position)

Slumber Song

(to the tune of "Jesus Loves Me")

Let's tuck you in, turn off the light—
now it's time to say "Good night."
God is watching over you,
he keeps us safe the whole night through.

Chorus:
God's love is near us,
God's love is near us,
God's love is near us,
sleep tight, I love you, dear.

I go to bed
and sleep in peace.
Lord, only you keep me safe.

Psalm 4:8

God Made the World

God said, "I made the earth." Isaiah 45:12

Who made the world?
God made the world!
God made light and God made air.
God made green plants everywhere.
And it was good.
What do you see in the world?

Who made the world?
God made the world!
God made the fish.
God made the sky.
God made animals and people, oh my!
And it was good.
What do you see in the world?

How many swishy fish do you see?

Who made the world?
God made the world!
God made the world.
God made it the best.
Then what did God make?
God made REST.
And it was very good.
Night-night!

Count the stars in the sky.

Quiet Time

Night-Light has some questions.
Help him find the answers.

- Who made the world?
- What did God say?
    "I made the earth."
- How can you thank God for the
    world?

Prayer Time

Let's thank our God for all his love
and watchful care from up above.

Dear God,
Thank you for the wondrous world
you made with so much love.
Thank you for the earth below
and for the stars above.
Amen.

Sleep Time

Tonight's Bible word is **world**.
God's world is so great. What's
your favorite part of the world?
Sleep tight!

Adam Names the Animals

God said, "I have called you by name." Isaiah 43:1

Who made the world? God made the world!
Who made trees and flowers?
God made trees and flowers!
Who made animals?
God made animals!
What else did God make?
God made a man!
God loved the man and named him "Adam."
God gave Adam a special job.
What do you think it was?

God told Adam to name the animals.
But—oh my! Look at all the animals!
Fuzzy, furry, tiny, tall—
how could Adam name them all?
"Elepottamus"? "Kangamoo"?
What should he call them? What would you do?

Find the elephant and the kangaroo.

Adam gave names to all the animals.
Can you point to the animals and call them by name?
Adam named the animals, and God was pleased.
Then God gave Adam a helper.
Adam named her "Eve."
Everyone had a special name.
Did you know God has a special name for you?
God calls you—his!

Point to Adam and Eve. Find a red flower.

Quiet Time

Night-Light has some questions.
Help him find the answers.

- What job did God give Adam?
- What did God say?
    "I have called you by name."
- What is your name?

Prayer Time

Let's thank our God for all his love
and watchful care from up above.

Dear God,
Thank you for your love
and for sending it from up above.
We're glad you gave us each a name
and love all of us the same!
Amen.

Sleep Time

Tonight's Bible word is **name**.
Think about your nice name and
all the special names of your
family and friends. Good night.

Noah Obeys God

God said, "Obey me." Jeremiah 7:23

God looked at the earth.
He saw people everywhere disobeying him.
The people didn't love God.
They didn't do anything God said.
God was very sad.
Did anyone love God?
Yes! Noah loved God!

God would make it rain and rain.
God would wash the world clean.
But God loved Noah and would keep him safe.
"Build a boat," said God. So Noah obeyed God.
Zzz-zzz—bang-bang-BANG!
Noah built a big boat called an ark.
God sent special guests to ride in the ark.
Who were they?
Fuzzy, fluffy, feathery, friendly animals!
God sent every kind of animal.

What animals do you see?

Into the ark went the animals.
Into the ark went Noah and his family.
Then whump! God closed the door.
God made it rain and rain.
God washed the earth clean.
But God kept Noah and his family
and all the animals safe and sound.
Drip, drip, drop—
God's love will never stop!

Point to Noah. Find the turtles.

Quiet Time

Night-Light has some questions.
Help him find the answers.

- Why did Noah obey God?
- What did God say?
  "Obey me."
- Who can you obey?

Prayer Time

Let's thank our God for all his love
and watchful care from up above.

Dear God,
We know you love us.
And we love you, too.
Please help us always obey you
in everything we do.
Amen.

Sleep Time

Tonight's Bible word is **obey**.
Think about how happy you feel when
you obey God. Night-night!

God's Promise

God said, "What God promises, he keeps." Numbers 23:19

Drip, drop, pouring down—
rain was falling all around!
God promised to wash the world clean.
And God promised to keep Noah, his family,
and the animals safe in the ark—and God did.
God always keeps his promises!
But there was so much water!
Drip, drip, drop—
would the rain ever stop?

Yes! God promised to stop the rain—
and God always keeps his promises.
God stopped the rain.
Then God sent a wind to blow across the water.
Ooo-ooo! The wind blew and blew.
It swirled and whirled all around,
and the flood began to go down, down, down—
just as God had promised!

Find a fish and a frog.

Noah opened the window.
The sunshine came in and a dove flew out.
Noah sent the pretty bird to find dry land.
Guess what the bird found!
The bird found a green leaf!
Noah knew there was dry land.
Noah was thankful to God.
God had kept his promise!

What does the dove have in his beak?

Quiet Time

Night-Light has some questions.
Help him find the answers.

- Who stopped the rain?
- What did God say?
    "What God promises, he keeps."
- Who always keeps his promises?

Prayer Time

Let's thank our God for all his love
and watchful care from up above.

Dear God,
Thank you for your promises—
each one you always keep.
Promise now to keep me safe
tonight while I'm asleep.
Amen.

Sleep Time

Tonight's Bible word is **promise**.
Think about God's promise of love.
Sleep tight!

Noah Thanks God

God said, "Show thanks to God." Psalm 50:14

The flood was finished.
The world was clean.
Noah was thankful for dry land.
Noah was thankful everyone on the ark was safe.
And Noah was thankful they could come out of the ark!
The door opened up—CRRREAK—
then what a parade there was!

Lions, tigers, zebras, too—
Hippity-hop, Mr. Kangaroo!
Look at the sun shining up above—
let's thank God with all our love!
And that's just what Noah did!
Can you say, "Thank you, God"?

What animals do you see in the parade?

Oh! Look in the sky—
what do you see?
God set a rainbow in the sky.
God gave us the rainbow as a promise.
He promised never to flood the world again.
Isn't it wonderful that God always keeps his promises?
Let's thank God for his promises!

Name the rainbow colors. What is Noah doing?

Quiet Time

Night-Light has some questions.
Help him find the answers.

- Why was Noah thankful?
- What did God say?
  "Show thanks to God."
- How can we thank God?

Prayer Time

Let's thank our God for all his love
and watchful care from up above.

Dear God,
We want to thank you
for all you are and all you do;
for your great care and love so deep,
for your angels as we sleep.
Amen.

Sleep Time

Tonight's Bible word is **thank-you**.
Think about all the things you can
thank God for. Night-night!

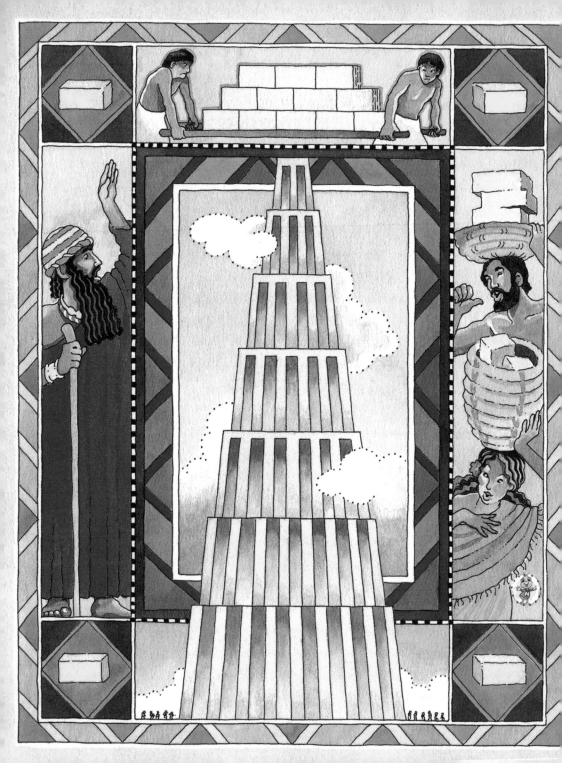

The Oh-No Tower

God said, "Remember that I am God." Isaiah 46:9

Long ago, people thought they were very smart.
They said, "There's no one smarter than us, not one!
We're smarter than God—or anyone!"
But were they smarter than God?
Oh, no! God is smarter than anyone.

The people wanted to be like God.
So they built a tall, tall, touch-the-sky tower.
Up and up they piled the bricks.
And as they worked, they said,
"There's no one wiser than us, not one!
We're wiser than God—or anyone!"
But were they wiser than God?
Oh, no! God is wiser than anyone.

Find the tower and a blue flower.

The tower was tall.
The people were happy.
But was God happy?
Oh, no!
God came down and scrambled the people's words around.
The people could not understand each other.
They spread out.
They went all about!
The people learned that no one is wiser than God.
Oh, yes!

Find two running mice.

Quiet Time

Night-Light has some questions.
Help him find the answers.

- What did the people say?
- What did God say?
    "Remember that I am God."
- Who is wiser than anyone?

Prayer Time

Let's thank our God for all his love
and watchful care from up above.

Dear God,
You're the wisest in every way.
We will follow you each day.
Amen.

Sleep Time

Tonight's Bible word is **wise**.
Think about how wise God is and how
he helps us every day. Sleep tight!

43

Abraham Trusts God

God said, "They will trust in the Lord." Zephaniah 3:12

Abraham and Sarah lived in a comfy-cozy house.
One day, God told Abraham to move to a new land.
God would lead the way.
Abraham didn't want to move.
But Abraham trusted God.
What do you think Abraham did?

Abraham packed!
Abraham packed this, Sarah packed that—
they took all their clothes and their little white cat.
Then march, march, march—
Abraham and Sarah followed God.
And they trusted God, too.
What a parade it was!

Point to Abraham and Sarah. Find the cat.

God led Abraham and Sarah to a new land.
God was happy that Abraham trusted him.
Abraham looked up. What did he see?
Trillions of twinkly stars!
Then God promised Abraham that his family
would be as many as the stars in the sky.
That's a big family!
Thank you, God.

Point to the tent. Who is in the tent?

Quiet Time

Night-Light has some questions.
Help him find the answers.

- Who did Abraham trust?
- What did God say?
    "They will trust in the Lord."
- Who can you trust?

Prayer Time

Let's thank our God for all his love
and watchful care from up above.

Dear God,
We know you love us so.
Please help our trust in you to grow.
Amen.

Sleep Time

Tonight's Bible word is **trust**.
Think about how nice it feels to trust
God and know he loves us.
Good night!

A Baby for Sarah

God said, "What God promises, he keeps." Numbers 23:19

Abraham and Sarah were sad.
They wanted a baby.
They wanted a baby to cuddle and love.
God promised Abraham
that his family would be as many as the stars,
but still there was no baby.
Poor Abraham and Sarah.

One day, three special guests came to visit.
The guests told Sarah she would have a baby.
Sarah smiled.
Sarah grinned.
Then Sarah laughed.
"I'm too old for babies!" Sarah laughed with a wink.
Will God keep his promise?
What do you think?

How many guests are visiting Abraham and Sarah?

Look—a baby! God kept his promise.
God gave Abraham and Sarah
a baby boy to cuddle and love.
They named the baby Isaac.
Then Abraham and Sarah thanked
God for keeping his promise.
What a happy family!

Point to baby Isaac. Where is a happy bird?

Quiet Time

Night-Light has some questions.
Help him find the answers.

- What did God promise Abraham and Sarah?
- What did God say?
    "What God promises, he keeps."
- Who keeps his promises to you?

Prayer Time

Let's thank our God for all his love and watchful care from up above.

Dear God,
Thank you for your promises—
we know they all come true.
That's because you love us all,
and we love you, too!
Amen.

Sleep Time

Tonight's Bible word is **promises**.
Think about God's promises and how much he loves you. Night-night!

Baby in a Basket

God said, "I will save you." Jeremiah 30:10

Baby Moses needed a safe place to hide.
But where?
Mother and Miriam, Moses' sister, thought and thought.
Mother got an idea!
She wove a grassy basket bin to put her precious baby in!
What did Mother do then?

Mother put baby Moses in his cozy basket.
Then she set the basket in the tall, cool grass by the river.
Miriam peeked through grass
to make sure baby Moses was safe.
Peekaboo!
We see you, baby Moses!
Oh! Someone's coming!
Who could it be?

Find baby Moses. Point to Miriam.

A princess!
The princess picked up the precious baby.
Miriam asked the princess if she wanted help with the baby.
Who did Miriam get to help?
Baby Moses' mother!
Everyone was so happy.
Mother and Miriam and Moses could be together again.
"Sleep tight, baby Moses," Mother said.
"I'll cuddle you and stay right here,
and God will keep you safe, my dear!"

Point to the princess. Where is Mother?

Quiet Time

Night-Light has some questions.
Help him find the answers.

- Where did Mother hide Moses?
- What did God say?
    "I will save you."
- How do you feel when God keeps
    you safe?

Prayer Time

Let's thank our God for all his love
and watchful care from up above.

Dear God,
Our Father up above,
you keep us safe with all your love.
We don't ever have to fear
because you are always near.
Amen.

Sleep Time

Tonight's Bible word is **safe.**
Think about how good it is to know God
watches over us. We're safe because God
loves us. Sleep tight!

Moses—God's Helper

God said, "You may serve me." Jeremiah 15:19

Moses had a long beard and a scratchy robe.
Moses had a flock of sheep and a shepherd's staff.
But the most important thing Moses had
was a heart of love for God.
Moses loved God more than anything!
One day, Moses saw a bright glow
on the side of the mountain.
"Oh me, oh my—what can it be?
I'll climb up the mountain to see what I see!"
What do you think Moses saw?

Moses saw a bush with fiery flames—
but the bush did not burn up!
Then Moses heard someone say his name.
Who talked to Moses?
God talked to Moses.
What do you think he said?

Point to the burning bush. Find Moses' sandals.

God told Moses he had an important job to do.
God told Moses to set his people free from the mean king.
God told Moses to be his special helper.
Then what did Moses say?
Moses said, "I'll be God's helper—special and true.
I'll do all the things God tells me to do.
I know God will help me wherever I go.
Being God's helper says, 'I love God so!'"

Point to the sheep. Find a fuzzy caterpillar.

Quiet Time

Night-Light has some questions.
Help him find the answers.

- Who talked to Moses?
- What did God say?
  "You may serve me."
- How can you be God's special
  helper and serve him?

Prayer Time

Let's thank our God for all his love
and watchful care from up above.

Dear God,
I want to obey you
and be your special helper, too.
Amen.

Sleep Time

Tonight's Bible word is **helper**.
Think about the ways you can be God's
special helper. Good night.

Red Sea Run

God said, "I will save you." Jeremiah 30:10

Once there was a mean king.
He didn't like God's people.
And he didn't like God.
What a nasty king he was!
But God loved his people and would keep them safe.
So God told Moses to lead his people
away from the mean king.
The mean king was angry and chased them!
Run, Moses, run—lead God's people free!
Run, Moses, run—but what about the sea?

The Red Sea was very big.
The Red Sea was very deep.
How could they get across?
How could God's people get safely to the other side?
Run, Moses, run—lead God's people free!
Run, Moses, run—but what about the sea?
Could the sea stop God? No, sirree!

Point to the mean king. Who is wearing a red robe?

God did an amazing thing.

WHOOSH!—God split the sea in half!

Moses and God's people walked safely to the other side.

Then Moses thanked God for keeping them safe.

Walk, Moses, walk—God set you free.

God can do anything—yes, sirree!

Point to the happy lamb. Find a big yellow fish.

Quiet Time

Night-Light has some questions.
Help him find the answers.

- Who split the Red Sea?
- What did God say?
    "I will save you."
- Who keeps you safe?

Prayer Time

Let's thank our God for all his love
and watchful care from up above.

Dear God,
Thank you for your power and
your awesome might.
You keep us safe
both day and night.
Amen.

Sleep Time

Tonight's Bible word is **safe**.
Think about God's love and how he
keeps us safe. Sleep tight!

God Gives Us What We Need

God said, "I will answer you." Jeremiah 33:3

God loved Moses.
And God loved his people.
But when God helped them escape from the nasty king,
the people didn't say, "Thank you, God."
The people grumbled and groaned.
They mumbled and moaned.
"We're hungry!" they said.
"We want something to eat! Doesn't God love us?"

Yes, God loves us all.
And God gives us what we need.
So God sent the people something yummy to eat.
What did God send?
God sent manna!
God sent his people delicious bread from heaven.
Manna was flaky, manna was sweet.
Yum-yummy manna—God's special treat!

Point to two hungry children. Find the manna.

Every morning and every night,
God sent food for his people to eat.
God gave his people manna when they were hungry.
God always gives us what we need.
Why?
Because God loves us!
Can you think of all the things God gives you?

What are the children gathering? Find a ladybug.

Quiet Time

Night-Light has some questions.
Help him find the answers.

- What did the people need?
- What did God say?
  "I will answer you."
- How can you thank God for
  answering your needs?

Prayer Time

Let's thank our God for all his love
and watchful care from up above.

Dear God,
Thanks so much
for all you give
to help us grow and
love and live.
Amen.

Sleep Time

Tonight's Bible word is **give**.
Think about all the special things God
gives us. Night-night!

God's Ten Rules

God said, "Obey me." Jeremiah 7:23

Moses loved God.
And Moses obeyed God.
When God called Moses up the mountain, Moses obeyed.
When God told Moses to speak to the people, Moses obeyed.
And when God told Moses to listen, Moses obeyed.

What did God tell Moses?
God gave Moses ten special rules to obey.
God told us he is God and we should worship only him.
God told us to love him and respect his name.
God told us to take a day of rest.
God told us to love our mommies and daddies.
God told us never, never to hurt anyone.
God told us husbands and wives should be true to each other.
God told us not to steal or ever tell a lie.
And God told us to be happy with what we have.
Then God wrote his rules on two stone tablets.
What good rules to obey!

How many stone tablets do you see?

Why did God give us special rules?
God gave us rules because he loves us.
God gave us rules to keep us safe and happy.
And God gave us his special rules to obey.
When we obey God's rules, we show that we love God.
Thank you, God!
Thank you for your special rules!

Find a yellow flower. Point to a bird in a nest.

Quiet Time

Night-Light has some questions.
Help him find the answers.

- What did God give us?
- What did God say?
   "Obey me."
- Whose special rules can you obey?

Prayer Time

Let's thank our God for all his love
and watchful care from up above.

Dear God,
Your rules help us every day.
Help us to trust them and obey.
Amen.

Sleep Time

Tonight's Bible word is **rules**.
Think about rules that keep us safe and
how happy God is when we obey him.
Good night!

God Helps Joshua

God said, "I will help you." Isaiah 41:10

Joshua was God's brave soldier.
Joshua knew God would always help him.
There was a city called Jericho.
The people there didn't love God.
So God decided to give Jericho to Joshua and his people.
But my, oh my!
There was a big, tall, can't-get-over-it wall around the city!
How could Joshua get over that wall?
God would help!

God told Joshua, all the soldiers, and all the priests
to march around the wall.
Right foot, left foot—step, step, step!
God told them to march around the wall seven times.
Round and round they all marched. 1, 2, 3, 4, 5, 6, 7!
Then God told them to blow their horns.
Tootle, toot—what a sound!
Tootle, toot—and the walls fell . . .

Point to Joshua. Find the tall wall.

DOWN!
Tumble tower, tumble down—
till every brick is on the ground!
God brought that tall wall down!
Joshua, all the soldiers, and all the priests
shouted with joy to God.
God had helped them!
And God helps us, too.
Thank you, God!

How many bricks are tumbling down?

Quiet Time

Night-Light has some questions.
Help him find the answers.

- What did God tell Joshua to do?
- What did God say?
    "I will help you."
- Who always helps us?

Prayer Time

Let's thank our God for all his love
and watchful care from up above.

Dear God,
We're glad you're always there
to help us out because you care!
Amen.

Sleep Time

Tonight's Bible word is **help**.
Think about how God helps you
and loves you. Night-night!

Ruth and Naomi Are Friends

God said, "Love your neighbor." Leviticus 19:18

Ruth and Naomi were good friends.
They shared a house.
And they shared the work.
Ruth swept the floors while Naomi washed the dishes.
And Naomi shared God with Ruth.
Naomi told Ruth all about God's love.
And soon, Ruth loved God as much as Naomi did.

Then one day, something sad happened.
Ruth and Naomi were left alone.
Their husbands had died.
What should they do?
Where should they go?
Naomi wanted Ruth to go back home
to live with her family.
But would Ruth go?

Find a grasshopper. Point to Ruth's broom.

Oh, no!
Ruth loved Naomi and wanted to stay with her.
Ruth knew that God brings us good friends,
and friends stick together.
So Ruth stayed with Naomi.
Ruth and Naomi were friends forever!

Count the dogs. Where is a circle shape?

Quiet Time

Night-Light has some questions.
Help him find the answers.

- Who brings us good friends?
- What did God say?
    "Love your neighbor."
- How can you thank God for your
    friends?

Prayer Time

Let's thank our God for all his love
and watchful care from up above.

Dear God,
We thank you for our friends.
Please help us
share and care for them.
Amen.

Sleep Time

Tonight's Bible word is **friends**.
Think about the good friends God has
given you. Good night, friend!

Samuel Listens to God

God said, "Listen to me." Isaiah 51:1

Samuel was a little boy who loved God.
Samuel lived in the temple with Eli the priest.
Samuel liked the temple.
He had good food. He learned about God.
And Samuel even had a comfy little mat to sleep on.
One night, Samuel was sound asleep.
He heard someone call his name—"Samuel. Samuel!"
Who was calling Samuel? Was it Eli?

"It wasn't me," said Eli. "Close your eyes and go to sleep."
So Samuel went to sleep.
But soon—"Samuel. Samuel!"
Who was calling Samuel? Was it Eli?
"It wasn't me," said Eli. "Close your eyes and go to sleep."
So Samuel lay down again.
But soon—"Samuel. Samuel!"
Who was calling Samuel? Was it Eli?

Point to Samuel and Eli.

No, it was God!
God talked to Samuel and Samuel talked to God.
"Speak, God, I am listening," said Samuel.
Samuel listened to God—then Samuel went to sleep.
Sleep well, Samuel!
God has special work for you to do!

Where are the moon and stars?

Quiet Time

Night-Light has some questions.
Help him find the answers.

- Who called Samuel's name?
- What did God say?
  "Listen to me."
- Who loves us just as he loved
  Samuel?

Prayer Time

Let's thank our God for all his love
and watchful care from up above.

Dear God,
Please help me listen to you
wherever I am, whatever I do.
Amen.

Sleep Time

Tonight's Bible word is **listen**.
Think about how important
it is to listen to God. Good night.

God Chooses David

God said, "The Lord looks at the heart." 1 Samuel 16:7

God wanted to choose a new king.
God would choose a king who loved him.
And God would choose a king who was strong and wise—
no matter his size!
So God sent Samuel to Jesse's family to choose the king.
There were eight brothers that God could use.
Only one would be king—
who would God choose?

The tall one with the wavy red hair?
Or the big, BIG brother who was standing there?
Would God choose the brother who was the oldest?
Or would he pick the thinnest or bravest or boldest?
Maybe the brother with new leather shoes?
Only one would be king—
who would God choose?

Point to the brother with red hair.

God chose David, the littlest brother!
God picked David because
David was wise and strong, and he loved God.
God didn't look at how small David was.
God looked at David's heart.
And David's heart was BIG!
His heart was filled with love for God.
Hooray for King David!

Point to David. Point to Samuel.

Quiet Time

Night-Light has some questions.
Help him find the answers.

- Who did God choose to be king?
- What did God say?
    "The Lord looks at the heart."
- How big is your love for God?

Prayer Time

Let's thank our God for all his love
and watchful care from up above.

Dear God,
We know you're very wise
to see our hearts and not our size.
Please help our faith in you to grow
as we choose to love you so.
Amen.

Sleep Time

Tonight's Bible word is **heart**.
Think about how God sees the love
in your heart. Night-night.

David and Goliath

God said, "I will make you strong." Isaiah 45:5

David had seven brothers.
David wasn't as big as his brothers.
And David wasn't as strong as his brothers.
David was the littlest brother of all!
But David loved God.
And David knew God was bigger and stronger
than anyone or anything. Yes, sirree!

Goliath was a big, BIG guy—and a meanie.
Goliath didn't love God.
Goliath laughed at God and said,
"No one's bigger or stronger than me!"
No, no, Goliath!
God is bigger and stronger than anyone!
David wanted to stop Goliath from laughing at God.
But David was so little—what could he do?

Point to the yellow robe. Find the blue helmet.

David asked for God's help.
Then David took a smooth stone from the ground.
He swung his sling round and round,
and—zing! plop!—Goliath fell down!
God helped David topple the mean giant.
Yeah, David! Yeah, God!
Let us clap and let us sing—
God is bigger than anything!

How many smooth stones do you see?

Quiet Time

Night-Light has some questions.
Help him find the answers.

- How did God help David?
- What did God say?
    "I will make you strong."
- Who is bigger and stronger than
    anything?

Prayer Time

Let's thank our God for all his love
and watchful care from up above.

Dear God,
We're glad you're who you are—
so big and full of might!
You keep us safe all day long
and in our sleep at night.
Amen.

Sleep Time

Tonight's Bible word is **strong**.
Think about how strong God is.
Night-night!

David Thanks God

God said, "Show thanks to God." Psalm 50:14

God always helped David and kept him safe.
David loved God and wanted to thank him.
But how could David say, "Thank you, God"?
David had an idea.
He could pray!
This is what David prayed:
"I love you, God.
You're stronger than anything and wiser than anyone.
The whole world is in your hands.
Thank you, God!"

But David wanted to thank God even more.
David had an idea.
He could play the harp!
David could play his little harp to thank God for his love.
This is what David played:
Plink, plinka-plink! Plinkity-plinkity-plink!

Find David's harp. How many yellow flowers do you see?

But David wanted to thank God even more!
David had an idea.
He could write a poem to God.
This is what David wrote: "Dear God, you are my shepherd.
You give me all I need. You help me and keep me safe.
I'm never afraid because you are with me.
You give me such good gifts, God!
I'm so happy that I'll be with you always. Thank you, God!"
David worshiped and thanked God for his love.
Thank you, God—we love you!

Find two lambs with black faces.

Quiet Time

Night-Light has some questions.
Help him find the answers.

- How did David thank God?
- What did God say?
  "Show thanks to God."
- How can you thank God?

Prayer Time

Let's thank our God for all his love
and watchful care from up above.

Dear God,
We're glad you're always there
and that you love us and you care.
Amen.

Sleep Time

Tonight's Bible word is **thanks**.
Think about the ways you can say,
"Thank you, God." Sleep tight.

Smart Solomon

God said, "I will give you wisdom." 1 Kings 3:12

Solomon was David's son. He loved God very much.
He became the king of God's people.
One day, God told King Solomon
that he could have anything he wanted.
"Oh, boy!" thought Solomon. "Anything I want?"
King Solomon scratched his head and thought.
What did he want?
What would you want?

Shiny jewels? Money galore?
Golden coins to count and store?
Lots of friends? Leather shoes?
A big new house—what would he choose?
Then Solomon remembered something.
He remembered that he was king!
He was king over lots of people.
How could he help all those people?
Suddenly, Solomon knew what he wanted!

How many gold coins do you see?

Solomon wanted to be wise!
If King Solomon were wise, he could help lots of people.
Solomon asked God to make him very smart.
God was happy with Solomon's choice.
He gave Solomon great wisdom.
Then God gave King Solomon riches and honor, too.
King Solomon was wise for loving God!

Point to Solomon's crown. How many jewels do you see?

Quiet Time

Night-Light has some questions.
Help him find the answers.

- What did Solomon ask God?
- What did God say?
    "I will give you wisdom."
- How can loving God make you
    smart like Solomon?

Prayer Time

Let's thank our God for all his love
and watchful care from up above.

Dear God,
We know you're very wise—
help us be wise like you.
Guide us with your loving care
in everything we do.
Amen.

Sleep Time

Tonight's Bible word is **wise**.
Think about how wise it is to love
and follow God. Sleep tight.

Daniel Prays

God said, "I will answer you." Jeremiah 33:3

Daniel loved God very much. He prayed to God day and night.
Daniel worked hard and did great things in the kingdom.
King Darius saw Daniel's work and was happy.
He wanted to put Daniel in charge of his whole kingdom!
But some other men were jealous.
They didn't want Daniel to be in charge.
So they plotted and planned.
What do you think they did?

The men went to King Darius and said,
"O King Darius, you are so great and true.
People should pray only to you!"
So the jealous men had King Darius write a law that said:
"NO PRAYING TO GOD FOR 30 DAYS."
But Daniel loved God and kept praying every day.
When King Darius heard this, he was sad.
Because of the law, he would have to punish Daniel.
Do you know what the punishment was?

Point to Daniel. Point to King Darius.

Daniel was tossed in the lions' den with growly-scowly lions!
Daniel was afraid, but Daniel kept praying to God.
Daniel said, "Dear God, I'll always pray to you
no matter what men say or do!"
As Daniel prayed, the lions growled and scowled and snarled!
But God answered Daniel's prayers.
God sent an angel to close the lions' mouths.
Then King Darius knew God is more powerful than anything!
King Darius told all the people to pray to God.
And what did Daniel do then? He prayed! Thank you, God!

How many growly lions do you see?

Quiet Time

Night-Light has some questions.
Help him find the answers.

- Who kept praying to God?
- What did God say?
    "I will answer you."
- When can you pray?

Prayer Time

Let's thank our God for all his love
and watchful care from up above.

Dear God,
We bow our heads to pray
and say we love you every day.
Amen.

Sleep Time

Tonight's Bible word is **pray.**
Think about how good it is to pray
to God. Night-night.

Brave Queen Esther

God said, "Be strong and brave." Joshua 1:7

Esther was a very beautiful lady.
She was a Jew, one of God's people.
Esther loved God very much.
The king chose Esther to be his queen.
Esther was glad to be queen, but one thing made her sad.
Haman was the king's helper.
He didn't love God and he didn't love God's people.
Haman even wanted to hurt God's people!
Naughty, naughty, Haman!

Queen Esther had to save God's people.
She had to tell the king about Haman.
But Esther was very afraid!
What if the king became angry with her?
Queen Esther loved God.
She wanted to help God's people.
But would God help Esther?

Find some grapes. Who is wearing a crown?

He did!
God helped Queen Esther be brave and courageous.
She told the king and guess what!
The king wasn't angry with Esther at all.
He was angry with Haman!
Queen Esther had saved God's people.
Hooray for brave Queen Esther!
Hooray for God!

Find a mouse and a happy cat.

Quiet Time

Night-Light has some questions.
Help him find the answers.

- Who did Queen Esther help?
- What did God say?
  "Be strong and brave."
- Who helps us be brave and
  courageous?

Prayer Time

Let's thank our God for all his love
and watchful care from up above.

Dear God,
You're with us all day long.
Please help us be
brave and strong.
Amen.

Sleep Time

Tonight's Bible word is **brave**.
Think about how strong and brave
we can be with God's help.
Good night.

God Answers Jonah

God said, "I will answer you." Jeremiah 33:3

The people of Nineveh didn't obey God.
God told Jonah to tell the people, "Obey me."
But what did Jonah say? "Oh, no! I won't go!"
Jonah did not want to talk to the mean people.
So Jonah ran and hid from God.
No, no, Jonah! You can't hide from God!

Jonah jumped into the sea. Kersplash!
He sank down, down, down, until—glip-glup—
a big fish swallowed him up!
For three days and nights, Jonah sat in the belly of the fish.
It smelled pretty awfulish!
Jonah was sorry he'd disobeyed,
so Jonah just sat there and prayed and prayed.
Jonah told God he was sorry.
Jonah thanked God for saving his life.
And Jonah told God he loved him.
But did God answer Jonah's prayers?

Point to the starfish. What is Jonah doing?

Yes, he did!
God always answers our prayers.
God made the big fish spit Jonah out on the sand—pftuwee!
Jonah was safe!
Jonah was thankful that God answers our prayers.
What did Jonah do then?
He jumped up and ran to Nineveh.
Jonah obeyed God!

How many seashells are there?

Quiet Time

Night-Light has some questions.
Help him find the answers.

- What did Jonah do in the fish?
- What did God say?
     "I will answer you."
- Who will answer your prayers?

Prayer Time

Let's thank our God for all his love
and watchful care from up above.

Dear God,
Each time we pray to you,
we know you'll hear
and answer, too.
Amen.

Sleep Time

Tonight's Bible word is **answers**.
Think about how God hears
and answers all your prayers.
Night-night.

Happy Birthday, Jesus!

God said, "I am with you." Jeremiah 30:11

What a quiet night it was!
Mary and Joseph walked along the road.
Mary smiled. She knew God's promise was near.
Mary knew that the baby she would have
was God's greatest promise.
But Mary was tired. So was Joseph.
Yawwwn!

After a while, they came to the town of Bethlehem.
Where could they rest?
Where could the special baby be born?
Joseph asked if there were any rooms.
"No room, no room," said the innkeeper.
Everywhere Joseph looked, it was the same.
No room here, no room there.
But God was watching—he would care.
And he did. God led them to a cozy stable.
Then late that night, just before morn . . .

Point to the brown donkey. How many stars do you see?

115

God's tiny baby Son was born!
Mary wrapped him in a blanket tight,
and Jesus slept in a manger that night.
In that still quiet night, God sent his Son to us.
God promised the world a Savior and Prince of Peace.
And God always keeps his promises!
Jesus came to save us.
Jesus came to give us peace.
And Jesus came to love us.
Happy birthday, Jesus! We love you, too.

Point to the manger. How many animals do you see?

Quiet Time

Night-Light has some questions.
Help him find the answers.

- Who sent Jesus to us?
- What did God say?
    "I am with you."
- How can you tell Jesus you
    love him?

Prayer Time

Let's thank our God for all his love
and watchful care from up above.

Dear God,
Thank you for sending
your Son from above.
Jesus is our Prince of Peace
and the one we love.
Amen.

Sleep Time

Tonight's Bible word is **Jesus**.
Think about the special night when
Jesus was born and how much God
loves us. Sleep tight.

Where's Jesus?

Jesus said, "Learn from me." Matthew 11:29

As Jesus grew up, he learned more and more about God.
Jesus learned about God, his Father.
God gave Jesus great wisdom and love.
One day, Mary and Joseph took Jesus to the big city.
They went to Jerusalem for a special festival.
It was a time to honor and thank God for his love.
The city was busy, busy, busy.
When it was time to go home,
Mary and Joseph couldn't find Jesus!
Where was Jesus?

Mary and Joseph were so worried—
back and forth they searched and scurried!
They looked for Jesus in the square.
They searched for Jesus everywhere.
But they couldn't find him anywhere!
Where was Jesus?

Point to the kitten.

There he is!
Jesus was in the temple.
Jesus was talking with the teachers.
What were they talking about?
They were talking about God!
Jesus was asking questions and giving answers.
People were learning about God.
Jesus was happy to be talking about God.
And Joseph and Mary were happy to find Jesus!

Point to the teachers. Find a red hat.

Quiet Time

Night-Light has some questions.
Help him find the answers.

- Where was Jesus?
- What did Jesus say?
    "Learn from me."
- How can you learn about God?

Prayer Time

Let's thank our God for all his love
and watchful care from up above.

Dear God,
Please help us learn about you—
about the Bible and Jesus, too.
Amen.

Sleep Time

Tonight's Bible word is **learn**.
Think about how happy God is when
we learn about him. Night-night.

Jesus Is Baptized

Jesus said, "Do all things that are right." Matthew 3:15

One day, Jesus went to the Jordan River.
What did Jesus see?
Jesus saw a man baptizing people in the water.
That man was John the Baptist.
His clothes were made of camel's hair.
He was talking to the people there.
John told the people they had done wrong things.
John told the people they should be sorry.
And John told the people they could tell God they were sorry
by being baptized in the water.

Jesus wanted to be baptized. He walked into the water.
John the Baptist said, "Oh no, Jesus!
You should be baptizing me instead!"
But Jesus knew that God wants everyone to be baptized.
And Jesus always obeyed God.
So John baptized Jesus in the Jordan.
Then what did Jesus see?

Point to John the Baptist. Find two fish.

Jesus saw the Spirit of God!
God's Spirit came down from heaven like a dove
and rested on Jesus.
God said he was very happy with Jesus, his Son.
Then John the Baptist and everyone knew
that it was right to be baptized.
We make God happy when we obey him.
Just like Jesus did!

How many flowers do you see?

Quiet Time

Night-Light has some questions.
Help him find the answers.

- Who did Jesus obey?
- What did Jesus say?
    "Do all things that are right."
- How can we obey God?

Prayer Time

Let's thank our God for all his love
and watchful care from up above.

Dear God,
Jesus always obeyed you.
Please help us always obey, too.
Amen.

Sleep Time

Tonight's Bible word is **obey**.
Think about how Jesus obeyed God
and how we can obey him, too.
Good night.

Follow-Me Fishermen

Jesus said, "Follow me." Matthew 4:19

One day, Jesus was walking beside the Sea of Galilee.
Jesus saw many things.
Jesus saw boats and birds.
Jesus saw waves and water.
And Jesus saw fish and fishermen.

Two of the fishermen were brothers.
Peter and Andrew were catching fish in their nets.
They looked up and saw Jesus walking toward them.
Jesus looked at them and said,
"Come, follow me and I will make you fishers of men."
At once, Peter and Andrew dropped their fishing nets.
They wanted to go with Jesus.
They wanted to follow him and learn about God.
Where did they go?

How many fish are in the net?

They went to look.
They went to find more people who wanted
to know, love, and follow Jesus.
We can be like Peter and Andrew.
We can follow Jesus, too!
And we can tell other people about him!

What are Peter and Andrew doing?

Quiet Time

Night-Light has some questions.
Help him find the answers.

- Who were the two brothers?
- What did Jesus say?
  "Follow me."
- How can we know, love, and
  follow Jesus?

Prayer Time

Let's thank our God for all his love
and watchful care from up above.

Dear God,
Please help us follow you
in all we say and all we do.
Amen.

Sleep Time

Tonight's Bible word is **follow**.
Think about how we can follow
Jesus and learn about him.
Good night.

Love Everyone

Jesus said, "Love each other." John 13:34

Jesus came to love us.

Jesus came to teach us.

And Jesus came to teach us about love!

One day, Jesus was teaching many people on a hillside.

Look at all the people!

Everyone knew that Jesus was wise.

And everyone knew that Jesus taught God's truth.

What did Jesus teach them?

Jesus said to love everyone!

Jesus said to love all people no matter what they say or do.

Even the ones who never share? Yes!

Even the ones who pull our hair? Yes!

Even the ones who scowl and frown? Yes!

And even the ones who push us down? Yes! Yes! YES!

Jesus said to love other people as we love ourselves.

Find a woman holding a baby.

Jesus wants us to love all people
no matter what they say or do.
When we love others,
it shows Jesus that we love him, too.
So when you meet someone, here's what you can do—
shake hands, smile and say,
"Jesus and I love you!"

How many smiling people do you see?

Quiet Time

Night-Light has some questions.
Help him find the answers.

- Who does Jesus want us to love?
- What did Jesus say?
    "Love each other."
- How can you show love to others?

Prayer Time

Let's thank our God for all his love
and watchful care from up above.

Dear God,
You are so amazing!
Your love is like no other.
Please help us to be good and kind,
and show love to each other.
Amen.

Sleep Time

Tonight's Bible word is **love**.
Think about all the people you can
love and how you can love them the
way Jesus wants. Sleep tight.

Jesus Stops the Storm

Jesus said, "Don't be afraid." Matthew 10:31

One night, Jesus and his friends climbed into a boat.
Stars sparkled. The moon twinkled.
Waves rocked the little boat
back and forth, back and forth.
Yawwwn—Jesus was sleepy.
He lay down and fell fast asleep.
Shhh! Don't wake Jesus.

Then all of a sudden—boom, crash, BOOM!
What a storm!
The rain drummed—ratta-tat-tat!
The wind blew—ooo-ooo-ooo!
Water splashed into the boat.
Jesus' friends were afraid. They woke Jesus.
"What if we sink? What if we drown?
How can you sleep with the rain pouring down?"
What did Jesus do?

Point to the lightning. Can you blow like the wind?

Jesus said, "Wind, stop! Waves, stop!"
Did the wind and waves obey him? They did!
The waves stopped flowing.
The wind stopped blowing.
Everyone was safe.
Jesus' friends asked, "Who is this who can stop a storm?"
Who is this? It's Jesus!
Jesus keeps us safe so we don't have to be afraid.
Thank you, Jesus!

Point to a star. Find the moon.

Quiet Time

Night-Light has some questions.
Help him find the answers.

- How did Jesus help his friends?
- What did Jesus say?
    "Don't be afraid."
- Who keeps you safe?

Prayer Time

Let's thank our God for all his love
and watchful care from up above.

Dear God,
We're glad for Jesus' love
that you give to all you've made.
We know with Jesus by our side
we'll never be afraid.
Amen.

Sleep Time

Tonight's Bible word is **safe**.
Think about how God keeps you safe
all day and all night. Night-night!

Dinner for 5,000

Jesus said, "Help other people freely." Matthew 10:8

Look at all the people!
The people were listening to Jesus.
They were learning about God and his love.
But—grumble, grumble—their tummies were hungry!
Where could they eat? Where would they find food?
Jesus' friends were worried.
So many people, so many hungry tummies!
What would Jesus do?

Andrew saw a little boy with a food basket.
What's in the basket?
Tasty bread and yummy fish.
The little boy wanted to share his meal with Jesus.
What a nice little boy!
But how could five loaves of bread and two small fish
fill so many hungry, grumbly tummies?
What would Jesus do?

Count the loaves and fish.

Jesus thanked God for the food.
Then he divided it for all the people.
Jesus made the meal big enough to feed everyone.
Then what a picnic they had!
Yum-yummy, food filled every tummy!
Jesus fed all those hungry people with one little boy's meal.
The boy shared his food and his love, too!
Would you share your lunch with others?
Would you share your love with others?
What would Jesus do?

Find a spotted puppy. Find a yellow bird.

Quiet Time

Night-Light has some questions.
Help him find the answers.

- Who shared his food with Jesus?
- What did Jesus say?
  "Help other people freely."
- How can you help others?

Prayer Time

Let's thank our God for all his love
and watchful care from up above.

Dear God,
Please help us always share
and give to show we really care.
Amen.

Sleep Time

Tonight's Bible word is **give**.
Think about what you can give to
others to show them God's love.
Sleep tight.

141

The Good Samaritan

Jesus said, "Show mercy." Luke 6:36

Jesus told a story about a man who was robbed.
Mean men stole the man's money and
left him lying hurt in the road.
Ouch! The poor hurt man! Who would help him?
Step, step, step. A village priest came along,
but he didn't stop—he just went on!
There's a hurt man lying there,
but who will stop to offer care?

Step, step, step. A Levite man came along,
but he didn't stop—he just went on!
The Levite didn't help the man.
The priest didn't help the man.
Would anyone help him?
There's a hurt man lying there,
but who will stop to offer care?

Point to the hurt man.

Clip-clop, clippity-clop.
A Samaritan came riding on a donkey.
Clip-clop, clippity-clop.
The Samaritan was the one to stop!
The good Samaritan gave the man water to drink
and covered his wounds.
Then the good Samaritan took the hurt man to town
and paid for his care. What a nice man!
Jesus wants us to show we care
and help when someone needs us there.

Who is giving the man a drink? Where is the donkey?

Quiet Time

Night-Light has some questions.
Help him find the answers.

- Who helped the hurt man?
- What did Jesus say?
  "Show mercy."
- How can you show kindness and
  mercy to others?

Prayer Time

Let's thank our God for all his love
and watchful care from up above.

Dear God,
We're glad you're always there.
Help us show how much we care.
Amen.

Sleep Time

Tonight's Bible word is **mercy**.
Think about how happy Jesus is
when we're kind and show mercy
to others. Good night.

The Wise Builder

Jesus said, "Trust in me." John 14:1

Jesus told a story of two builders—
one was wise and one was not.
See if you can tell which builder was so smart.
The first builder built his house on sand—
slippery-groundy, slidey-downy sand. Uh-oh!
The other builder built his house on hard rock—
rough and rigid, really rugged rock. Ahhh!
When the builders were done, each thought
he was the best builder who ever built!
But then the rains came.

Whoooosh, whoosh—the rains came down,
and the house on the sand tumbled down to the ground!
But the house built on stone
didn't budge, bend, or moan!
That house stood stock-still on that rock on the hill!

Find a saw. How many nails do you see?

Who was the smartest builder?
The one who built his house on the rock!
When troubles came, the house stood firm and didn't fall.
Did you know that we're builders, too?
We can be wise builders when we build our lives on Jesus.
When we trust and love Jesus,
we can be strong like the house on the rock!

Point to the house on the rock.

Quiet Time

Night-Light has some questions.
Help him find the answers.

- Who was the wise builder?
- What did Jesus say?
    "Trust in me."
- Whose love can we trust?

Prayer Time

Let's thank our God for all his love
and watchful care from up above.

Dear God,
Please send help from up above
to build our lives on Jesus' love.
Amen.

Sleep Time

Tonight's Bible word is **build**.
Think about how good it is to build our
trust in Jesus. Sleep tight.

The Lost Sheep

Jesus said, "I will be with you always." Matthew 28:20

Jesus once told a story about a shepherd who had 100 sheep.
One day, the shepherd counted his sheep. "96, 97, 98, 99—
my, oh my! There's one I can't find!"
One of the sheep was lost!
The shepherd had many more sheep,
but he loved every one of them.
"I'll find my sheep—I'll look high and low.
But where should I start? I just don't know!"

The shepherd looked behind a stone,
he searched beside the brook.
The sad old shepherd searched the fields—
oh, where else should he look?
The shepherd looked up in a tree and behind a dandelion.
He searched and sought his little sheep—
he'd never stop his tryin'!
"Oh, can you help me find my lamb? I really love him so!
Do you see my little lamb? If so, please let me know!"

What animals do you see?

There he is!
The shepherd was so happy to find his little sheep,
that he whooped with joy—oh, boy!
He brought his sheep back to the flock,
then had a party to celebrate.
God is like that shepherd.
He wants us to stay close to him all the time.
Why? Because he loves us—every one!

How many dandelions do you see?

Quiet Time

Night-Light has some questions.
Help him find the answers.

- Why did the shepherd look for
    his lost sheep?
- What did Jesus say?
    "I will be with you always."
- Who wants you close to him?

Prayer Time

Let's thank our God for all his love
and watchful care from up above.

Dear God,
We want to be near you
and love you dear
our whole lives through.
Amen.

Sleep Time

Tonight's Bible word is **near**.
Think about how God wants to be near
you and how good it feels to be close to
God. Good night.

He Can Walk!

Jesus said, "Trust in me." John 14:1

Once there was a man who couldn't walk.
The man would lie on his mat all day and night.
The man's friends said, "Jesus can help you!"
The friends believed in Jesus and his power.
So they took the man to see Jesus.
Do you think Jesus helped him?
Let's see!

Jesus looked at the man who couldn't walk.
Jesus looked at the man's friends.
And Jesus saw their faith!
Jesus knew the friends believed in his power and love.
That made Jesus very happy!
Then Jesus said to the crippled man,
"You're forgiven. Get up, take your mat, and go home!"
What do you think happened then?

How many friends are with the crippled man?

The man stood up and walked!
The man who had never walked
could skip and jump and walk and run.
Everyone praised Jesus.
The people were very surprised—
but not the man's friends. They trusted Jesus.
They had faith in Jesus' power.
And they believed that Jesus could do anything.
We can trust and believe in Jesus, too!

Find a happy bird.

Quiet Time

Night-Light has some questions.
Help him find the answers.

- How did Jesus help the crippled man on the mat?
- What did Jesus say?
   "Trust in me."
- Who can do anything?

Prayer Time

Let's thank our God for all his love and watchful care from up above.

Dear God,
Please help us trust in you
and have more faith
our whole lives through.
Amen.

Sleep Time

Tonight's Bible word is **believe**.
Think about how much we trust and believe in Jesus' love. Night-night!

Jesus Loves Children

Jesus said, "Come to me." Matthew 19:14

Jesus was teaching the grown-ups.
Jesus was teaching them about love.
All the mommies and daddies wanted their
little girls and boys to be close to Jesus.
But Jesus' friends said,
"Oh, no—make them go! Jesus is too busy!"
What did Jesus say?

Jesus said, "Come to me."
Jesus wanted the little children near.
Jesus hugged the children and loved them.
Jesus wanted the little children to learn about God.
So all the children came to Jesus.
Big kids, small kids, freckled-nosed tall kids.
Sad kids, happy kids, giggling-wiggling glad kids.
Kids with black hair, kids with brown;
kids from every tent and town.
They all came to Jesus!

Which child has freckles?

Why did Jesus want the little children to come to him?
Because Jesus loves little children.
Jesus loves each boy and girl—
every child around the world!
And Jesus knows children love him, too.
Thank you, Jesus—we do love you!

How many children do you see?

Quiet Time

Night-Light has some questions.
Help him find the answers.

- Why did Jesus want little
    children to come to him?
- What did Jesus say?
    "Come to me."
- How do you tell Jesus you love him?

Prayer Time

Let's thank our God for all his love
and watchful care from up above.

Dear God,
Thank you for Jesus' love—
we love him so much, too.
Please help us find the ways to say,
"Jesus, we love you!"
Amen.

Sleep Time

Tonight's Bible word is **love**.
Think about how Jesus loves all little
children and how he loves you, too!
Sleep tight.

Zacchaeus Is Forgiven

Jesus said, "Forgive other people." Luke 6:37

Once there was a grump named Zacchaeus.
"Hummmph! No one likes me!" said Zacchaeus.
The people didn't like Zacchaeus because
he took their money for taxes.
Zacchaeus heard that Jesus was coming to town.
Everyone was happy. But Zacchaeus didn't understand.
"Hummph! Why does everyone love Jesus?
Guess I'll take a peek!" he said.
What did Zacchaeus do?

Zacchaeus climbed a tall tree!
He peeked through the branches.
When Jesus came to the tree, he said,
"Zacchaeus, come down. I'm going to your house."
Zacchaeus slid down the tree—zooop!
Everyone stared. Everyone was surprised!
Why would Jesus want to eat with grumpy Zacchaeus?

Find Zacchaeus. Point to Jesus.

Jesus ate with Zacchaeus because
Jesus loved Zacchaeus!
And Jesus forgave Zacchaeus for the mean things he'd done.
Do you know what happened then?
Zacchaeus was so happy.
He gave back the people's money.
Yeah, Zacchaeus!

How many shiny coins do you see?

Quiet Time

Night-Light has some questions.
Help him find the answers.

- Why did Jesus forgive Zacchaeus?
- What did Jesus say?
  "Forgive other people."
- Who can you forgive?

Prayer Time

Let's thank our God for all his love and watchful care from up above.

Dear God,
Thank you for forgiving us
for all the times we disobey.
Help us to forgive others
in the same special way.
Amen.

Sleep Time

Tonight's Bible word is **forgive.**
Think about people you can forgive
and how happy it makes God.
Night-night!

Give to God

Jesus said, "Give to God." Matthew 22:21

Jesus was at the temple with many people.
The people were thanking God for his love.
The people gave offerings and gifts to God.
What did the rich people give to God?
Gold and silver and precious jewels.
Clink, clink, clinkety-clink!
They gave much to God—but still had much left.

Then Jesus saw a poor widow.
She was dressed in tattered robes and her shoes had holes.
What could this poor woman give to God?
She had no gold or silver or precious jewels.
All she had were two copper coins—
Clink, clink!
The old woman had just two pennies to give,
but she gave everything to God.

Count the copper coins.

Who gave more to God—
the rich people or the poor woman?
The poor woman gave more to God!
Jesus said the poor woman gave more
because she gave all she had.
She gave out of her heart while
the other people gave out of their riches.
Jesus was proud of the woman—
and Jesus is proud when we give to God, too!

Point to the rich people. Point to the poor woman.

Quiet Time

Night-Light has some questions.
Help him find the answers.

- What did the woman give
  to God?
- What did Jesus say?
  "Give to God."
- What can you give to God?

Prayer Time

Let's thank our God for all his love
and watchful care from up above.

Dear God,
Please help us give to you
with everything we say and do.
Amen.

Sleep Time

Tonight's Bible word is **give.**
Think about all you can give to God.
Good night.

Jesus Is Coming!

Jesus said, "Be ready!" Luke 12:40

Everyone was excited.
Guess who was coming to town!
Jesus was coming! Jesus was coming to Jerusalem.
The people wanted to give Jesus a very special "hello."
Everyone scurried and hurried to get ready for Jesus.
"Hosanna, hosanna! Jesus is near!
But when will our Savior finally be here?
When you see Jesus, tell us he's near—
Clap your hands to say, 'Jesus is here!'"

The people laid their coats and robes along the road.
They wanted to make a special pathway for Jesus.
They wanted Jesus to know they loved him.
Then the people picked palm branches to wave.
They wanted Jesus to know he was special to them.
Oh, how they scurried to get ready for Jesus.
Hurry, hurry! Jesus could come any moment!

How many palm trees do you see?

Here's Jesus! Did you clap your hands?
All the people waved palm branches.
All the people praised Jesus.
All the people showed Jesus their love.
We can show Jesus our love, too.
"Hosanna, hosanna! Jesus is here!
He lives in our hearts and we feel him near!"
Clap your hands and tell Jesus true—
"Jesus, Jesus, we love you!"

What is Jesus riding on?

Quiet Time

Night-Light has some questions.
Help him find the answers.

- Who was coming to Jerusalem?
- What did Jesus say?
    "Be ready!"
- Who comes to live in our hearts?

Prayer Time

Let's thank our God for all his love
and watchful care from up above.

Dear God,
Thank you that Jesus is near
and that our hearts feel him here!
Help us be ready to tell him true—
"Jesus, we love you!"
Amen.

Sleep Time

Tonight's Bible word is **ready**.
Think about how you can always
be ready to love and follow Jesus.
Night-night.

Serve Each Other

Jesus said, "Be like the servant." Luke 22:26

It was supper time.
Jesus and his friends sat around the table.
It was a very special supper because
it would be Jesus' last supper with his friends.
Before they ate, Jesus did something surprising.
He took a towel and some water and then—
Jesus washed their feet!
He washed the dusty, dirty feet of all his friends.
When he was finished, he said,
"I have served you. Now you should serve each other."

Jesus' friends were so surprised!
They sat down at the table.
Then Jesus held up a cup to drink from and a loaf of bread.
Jesus blessed the cup and bread
and served his friends again.

How many pairs of sandals do you see?

Why did Jesus serve his friends in this special way?
Jesus wanted to show how much he loved them.
Jesus wanted his friends to serve others.
And Jesus wants us to serve others, too.
When we serve others and do kind things,
we show people we love them—
and we show Jesus we love him, too!
Friends and family, sister, brother—
Jesus said to serve each other!

Point to the cup and bread.

Quiet Time

Night-Light has some questions.
Help him find the answers.

- How did Jesus serve his friends?
- What did Jesus say?
  "Be like the servant."
- How can you serve others?

Prayer Time

Let's thank our God for all his love
and watchful care from up above.

Dear God,
Please help us find the way
to serve each other every day.
Amen.

Sleep Time

Tonight's Bible word is **serve.**
Think about all the people you can
serve and how you can be kind.
Sleep tight.

Jesus Died for Us

Jesus said, "Forgive them." Luke 23:34

Not everyone loved Jesus.
Not everyone believed that Jesus was God's Son.
Some of the people wanted to hurt him.
Jesus came to help us and teach us.
Jesus came to forgive us and heal us.
But most of all, Jesus came to love us.
Now the people wanted to hurt him.
But Jesus still loved the people.

They hung Jesus on a cross where he died.
Jesus' friends were very sad.
They knew he was God's Son.
They knew Jesus loved them.
But they didn't know why Jesus had to die.
"This is the saddest day—oh my!
Why did Jesus have to die?"
Do you know why?

Find Jesus' friends.

Jesus died for us!
He wants us to live in heaven with him forever.
But we can't get there on our own.
We need Jesus to take us home!
So Jesus died to forgive our sins
to show us God's love never ends.
We can be God's children, too—
Jesus died because he loves you!

How many friends have come to see Jesus?

Quiet Time

Night-Light has some questions.
Help him find the answers.

- Why did the people hurt Jesus?
- What did Jesus say?
    "Forgive them."
- How can you thank Jesus for his
    great love?

Prayer Time

Let's thank our God for all his love
and watchful care from up above.

Dear God,
We're glad that Jesus came
to love and forgive us
each the same.
Amen.

Sleep Time

Tonight's Bible word is **forgive**.
Think about Jesus' love and
how good it is to be forgiven.
Sleep tight.

Jesus Is Alive!

Jesus said, "I will be with you always." Matthew 28:20

Jesus' friends were sad.
It had been three days since Jesus died on the cross.
Several women who had followed Jesus came to visit the tomb.
The women walked along sadly.
My, how they missed Jesus!
Then suddenly, something amazing happened!

At the tomb, the big stone had been rolled away.
And what do you think they saw?
An angel! A lightning-bright angel!
The angel said,
"Don't be afraid. I know you're looking for Jesus—
but he's not here. Jesus is alive!"
The women peeked inside the tomb.
What did they see?

How many flowers do you see?

Nothing! The tomb was empty.
"Jesus is alive!" they shouted.
They were so happy that they ran to tell
Jesus' other friends the good news.
Jesus is alive today!
We're so happy, shout "Hooray!"
Jesus is alive today—
and forever!

How many happy friends do you see?

Quiet Time

Night-Light has some questions.
Help him find the answers.

- What did the women see?
- What did Jesus say?
    "I will be with you always."
- Who is alive today and forever?

Prayer Time

Let's thank our God for all his love
and watchful care from up above.

Dear God,
We're so thankful we can say,
"Jesus is alive today!"
Amen.

Sleep Time

Tonight's Bible word is **alive.**
Think about how happy we are that
Jesus is alive. Night-night.

185

Tell Others About Jesus

Jesus said, "Tell the Good News." Mark 16:15

Jesus' friends were so happy.
They knew that Jesus was God's Son.
They knew that Jesus was alive.
And they loved Jesus more than ever!
Jesus called to his friends and gathered them.
Jesus had something very important to tell them.
What do you think Jesus said?

Jesus told his friends to go all over the world.
Jesus told his friends to tell others
about his love and forgiveness.
And Jesus told his friends to baptize people
and help people to believe in God.
Then something amazing happened!

How many birds do you see? Count the fish.

Jesus was lifted up into the clouds!
Where was Jesus going?
Jesus was going to live in heaven with God!
Jesus' friends were so excited and happy.
They started doing what Jesus said right away.
Jesus' friends told everyone the good news about Jesus' love.
And they told about his amazing forgiveness!
How many people can you tell about Jesus?

Who is in the clouds?

Quiet Time

Night-Light has some questions.
Help him find the answers.

- What did Jesus tell his friends
  to do?
- What did Jesus say?
  "Tell the Good News."
- Who can tell about Jesus?

Prayer Time

Let's thank our God for all his love
and watchful care from up above.

Dear God,
Thank you for forgiving us
and giving us your Son.
Help us tell of Jesus' love
to everyone!
Amen.

Sleep Time

Tonight's Bible word is **tell.**
Think of all the people you can
tell about Jesus and his love.
Sleep tight.

Hello, Holy Spirit!

Jesus said, "Receive the Holy Spirit." John 20:22

Jesus promised to send us a special gift.
Jesus promised to send us a special friend and helper.
This helper is called the Holy Spirit.
Jesus' friends were waiting for the Holy Spirit.
They waited and they prayed.
When would the Holy Spirit come?
How would they know the Holy Spirit was here?
Oh, listen—someone is coming!

Whooosh! Suddenly there came the sound
of a big, BIG wind from heaven!
WHOOOSH! The sound filled the house
where Jesus' friends were sitting.
Then flashes like heavenly flames came down
and people started praising God.
"Is this our heavenly friend?
Is this the Holy Spirit Jesus said he would send?"

Point to someone praying.

Yes! It was the Holy Spirit!
The Holy Spirit came to help us do what Jesus wants us to do.
The Holy Spirit came to teach us more about God's love.
And the Holy Spirit came so we could
serve Jesus with love and courage!
Hello, Holy Spirit! We're so glad to meet you!

Find two water jugs.

Quiet Time

Night-Light has some questions.
Help him find the answers.

- Who is our special helper?
- What did Jesus say?
    "Receive the Holy Spirit."
- How can the Holy Spirit help you?

Prayer Time

Let's thank our God for all his love
and watchful care from up above.

Dear God,
We'll be thankful to the end
for the Holy Spirit—
our special friend.
Amen.

Sleep Time

Tonight's Bible word is **Holy Spirit**.
Think about our special friend,
the Holy Spirit, and how he helps us.
Good night.

Prayer Helps Peter

Jesus said, "Ask and you will receive." John 16:24

Peter was one of Jesus' friends.
He loved Jesus and wanted to tell others about him.
But a mean king didn't like Jesus and he didn't like Peter.
So the mean king tossed Peter in jail
and chained him to two rough, gruff guards.
Poor Peter.
How could he ever get free?

Many people loved Jesus and they loved Peter, too.
When they heard that Peter was in jail, what did they do?
They prayed!
They prayed and asked God to set Peter free.
Peter prayed, too—
then fell fast asleep between the two sleepy, snoring guards.
Shhh, be very quiet—God is at work!
How would God help Peter escape?

Point to Peter praying.

God sent an angel to Peter.
The angel told Peter to wake up.
Then the chains fell off Peter's wrists.
Tiptoe, off we go—
did the mean guards awake?
Oh no, no, no!
God heard the prayers of the people and helped Peter escape.
Then Peter was free to tell more people about Jesus.
Yeah, Peter! Yeah, God!

Find Peter's chains.

Quiet Time

Night-Light has some questions.
Help him find the answers.

- Why did God send the angel to help Peter?
- What did Jesus say?
    "Ask and you will receive."
- When do you pray?

Prayer Time

Let's thank our God for all his love and watchful care from up above.

Dear God,
We're glad you're always there
to listen to our every prayer.
Amen.

Sleep Time

Tonight's Bible word is **prayer**.
Think about how God hears and
answers our prayers. Night-night.

Our New Home

Jesus said, "I am making everything new!" Revelation 21:5

The Bible tells us what it will be like
to live with God and Jesus.
Everything will be new!
God will make a new heaven and a new earth.
God will send a new city down from heaven.
But what will the city be like?
Let's see!

Look, behold!
A city of gold, with gates of gleaming stone.
And there is Jesus, full of light, sitting on his throne!
The river of life flows from the throne,
along the streets of gold.
And there's truth and peace and
much more love than anyone can hold!

What colors do you see?

God will wipe away each tear.
There'll be no crying in that place!
No sorrow, no pain, no fear—
only love and joy and the light of God's face.
We'll greet each other with smiles and laughter.
With Jesus and God,
we'll live happily ever after!

How many smiling people do you see?

Quiet Time

Night-Light has some questions.
Help him find the answers.

- Who will be on the throne?
- What did Jesus say?
  "I am making everything new!"
- How will people feel living with
  Jesus and God?

Prayer Time

Let's thank our God for all his love
and watchful care from up above.

*Dear God,
Thank you for making
everything new—
and letting us live
with Jesus and you.
Amen.*

Sleep Time

Tonight's Bible word is **heaven.**
Think about how very beautiful
heaven will be. Night-night.

Scripture Index

"God said" verses

"I made the earth." *(Isaiah 45:12)* 21

"I have called you by name." *(Isaiah 43:1)*. 25

"Obey me." *(Jeremiah 7:23)* 29, 69

"What God promises, he keeps." *(Numbers 23:19)*. 33, 49

"Show thanks to God." *(Psalm 50:14)* 37, 93

"Remember that I am God." *(Isaiah 46:9)* 41

"They will trust in the Lord." *(Zephaniah 3:12)* 45

"I will save you." *(Jeremiah 30:10)*. 53, 61

"You may serve me." *(Jeremiah 15:19)*. 57

"I will answer you." *(Jeremiah 33:3)* 65, 101, 109

"I will help you." *(Isaiah 41:10)* 73

"Love your neighbor." *(Leviticus 19:18)* 77

"Listen to me." *(Isaiah 51:1)*. 81

"The Lord looks at the heart." *(1 Samuel 16:7)*. 85

"I will make you strong." *(Isaiah 45:5)* 89

"I will give you wisdom." *(1 Kings 3:12)* 97

"Be strong and brave." *(Joshua 1:7)*. 105

"I am with you." *(Jeremiah 30:11)* 115

"Jesus said" verses

"Learn from me." *(Matthew 11:29)* 119

"Do all things that are right." *(Matthew 3:15)* 123

"Follow me." *(Matthew 4:19)* 127

"Love each other." *(John 13:34)* 131

"Don't be afraid." *(Matthew 10:31)* 135

"Help other people freely." *(Matthew 10:8)* 139

"Show mercy." *(Luke 6:36)* 143

"Trust in me." *(John 14:1)* 147, 155

"I will be with you always." *(Matthew 28:20)* 151, 183

"Come to me." *(Matthew 19:14)* 159

"Forgive other people." *(Luke 6:37)* 163

"Give to God." *(Matthew 22:21)* 167

"Be ready!" *(Luke 12:40)* 171

"Be like the servant." *(Luke 22:26)* 175

"Forgive them." *(Luke 23:34)* 179

"Tell the Good News." *(Mark 16:15)* 187

"Receive the Holy Spirit." *(John 20:22)* 191

"Ask and you will receive." *(John 16:24)* 195

"I am making everything new!" *(Revelation 21:5)* 199

Susan L. Lingo has spent most of her life working with and writing for children of all ages. A former early childhood and elementary school teacher, Susan is the author of over forty-five Christian books and resources for kids, teachers, and parents. Now Susan's lively approach and age-appropriate style come together in this unique children's Bible, communicating God's Word in a way that preschoolers can understand—and remember! With *My Good Night Bible,* Susan hoped to create a cozy bedtime feel for parents and children to enjoy, while keeping God in the middle of each story. Susan and her husband reside in Loveland, Colorado, with their two children, Lindsay and Dane. When she's not busy creating great projects as the owner and operator of Bright Ideas Books™ and Book Production, Susan enjoys her cats, tennis, golf, reading, and of course, working with children.

Kathy Parks has been a fashion illustrator, courtroom artist, commercial artist, and the illustrator of over 200 music lesson books. Now the art of Kathy Parks lights up *My Good Night Bible,* her fourth book with Standard. Her goal for the book was "to create a sense of infinite variety within the structure of the main design, like the freedom one finds within the protective structure of God's love and law." An earnest student of the Bible, Kathy also enjoys teaching children in Sunday school. She and her husband, Jerry, reside in San Diego County, California, with their two children, Molly and Ryan.